You Know You Are Short When...

Norene Fritz

WestBow Press books may be ordered through booksellers or by contacting:

WestBow Press
A Division of Thomas Nelson & Zondervan
1663 Liberty Drive
Bloomington, IN 47403
www.westbowpress.com
1 (866) 928-1240

ISBN: 978-1-5127-0459-4 (sc)
ISBN: 978-1-5127-0537-9 (e)

Library of Congress Control Number: 2015911822

Print information available on the last page.

WestBow Press rev. date: 10/15/2015

Scripture taken from the Holy Bible, NEW INTERNATIONAL VERSION®. Copyright © 1973, 1978, 1984 by Biblica, Inc. All rights reserved worldwide. Used by permission. NEW INTERNATIONAL VERSION® and NIV® are registered trademarks of Biblica, Inc. Use of either trademark for the offering of goods or services requires the prior written consent of Biblica US, Inc.

WESTBOW
PRESS®
A DIVISION OF THOMAS NELSON
& ZONDERVAN

FOREWORD

This inspiring book by Norene addresses the insight and life of being short.

History is impacted by people who were short. Even though we hear our fill of short jokes and songs, many short people have influenced our lives. World leaders such as Mahatma Gandhi, James Madison, Genghis Khan, Queen Victoria, Mother Theresa and Martin Luther King Jr. are a few recognized names. Athletes like Diego Maradona, Spud Webb, Mary Lou Retton, and Yogi Berra were champions. Artists as Ludwig Van Beethoven, Wolfgang Amadeus Mozart, Pablo Picasso and Henri de Toulouse-Latrec, were world renowned. There are scientists, explorers and writers whom have changed our lives, such as Enrico Fermi, Yuri Gagarin, and Gus Grissom. Writers such as Truman Capote, J. R. R. Tolkien, Charlotte Bronte, John Keats and William Faulkner were important literary contributors. Mel Brooks, Dolly Parton, Michael J. Fox, Alfred Hitchcock, Sammy Davis, Jr., Elton John, Bob Dylan, Joe Pesci, Mickey Rooney, Rod Serling, and Paul Simon are a few whom have contributed to hours of enjoyment in the entertainment industry.

I would venture to say, that almost everyone who is short has been teased or ridiculed about their height with a tormenting laugh, a statement like, "It's just a joke." What people may fail to understand is that words do hurt. When the words sting, what do short people do? Just as the author of this book, they learn to smile and live with negative comments. They push themselves to succeed in life. How will they be affected? They might either let words destroy them or use the words to motivate them to higher and loftier goals. Just as the aforementioned examples of short people, they become very successful in their endeavors. They learn to overcome the obstacles. Norene is an excellent mother, grandparent and friend. She has earned a Master's Degree in Counseling, and has become a skilled and excellent therapist. She has opened her life to find God in her heart. She has shared her love, care and understanding, and given herself to others less fortunate. She is a remarkable person, who like so many other short people, have provided so much to others. She has learned to transform sarcastic jokes, harassment and ridicule into care and concern for others.

As a child my favorite movie was a science fiction flick called, "The Incredible Shrinking Man." The main character, Scott Carey, shrank from a full size man to the size of an atom by coming in contact with a mysterious fog. He provided a wonderful soliloquy which left a lasting impression on me. He said, "And then I meant something too. Yes, smaller than the smallest, I meant something too. To God there is no zero. I still exist!"

Richard Rizzo PhD. LP Licensed Psychologist

Founder and President of Primacare

(Mental Health Consultation Services)

Westland, Michigan

DEDICATION

"You Know You Are Short When..." is dedicated to all the short people who deserve to be recognized in a positive way.

It is dedicated in appreciation and love to the Great Potter, who loves us and knows why He created us to be short.

It is also dedicated to my parents who were short. I guess I would not be short without them.

ACKNOWLEDGEMENT

I would like to thank Danise Abbott, my illustrator, who worked with me through this project. Thank you for your patience, understanding and great talent.

Thank you Dr. Rizzo, for taking time to read my manuscript and sharing your forward through your expertise of understanding, helping people, and your kind words of encouragement.

I am grateful to all those who shared their personal life experiences of being short. You rock.

www.norenefritz.com

INTRODUCTION

"You Know You Are Short When..." is a fun, way to share episodes that happened to short people. The incidents are true, derived from various people of various ages. They shared the same experiences that I did.

This little book is for entertainment, but also to communicate what many short people hear and feel. I imagine very tall people go through the same thing, except with the opposite issues.

Trust me, I was not always tolerant of "short comments." Over the years I have learned to not just tolerate comments, but use them to help myself build character. I have learned to take those hurts to try and understand why people say what they say and act the way they act. I have learned to "turn lemons into lemonade."

"You Know You Are Short When..." will hopefully, help short people accept themselves as they are, and embrace how they are created, and use it to the best of their ability. Hopefully, "You Know You Are Short When..." will also help them to not be offended when someone makes an unwelcomed comment, but to roll with the punches, build self-esteem, change their self-image, and perspective of themselves and others.

Perhaps this book will help people be more aware, and more sensitive to people who are not exactly like them, whether they are too short, tall, fat, skinny, too dark or too light. It always amazes me and catches me off guard when people comment about my height, weight or nationality. I don't see myself as a height, weight or nationality. I just see myself as a person.

My hope is that people will see others as simply people, no matter where they are, whether in school, work, on the street, or wherever they are in life. Hopefully, too, this would take the edge off child/adult sarcasm or bullying. My advice is, think before you speak. Treat each other with respect; and treat them as you would have others treat you

A word fitly spoken is like apples of gold in pictures of silver. Proverbs 25:11 (KJV)

You know you are short when...

People tell you, you are.

You're SHORT!

Really?

Credit to Elizabeth Messing

Really?

~~~~~~~~~~~~~~~~

You know you are short when...

You are 60 years old and someone says, "Are you gonna grow?"

Duh!

~~~~~~~~~~~~~~~~~~~~~

You know you are short when...

You went to school with a guy 6'2" and someone laughs saying, "He grew up and you didn't".

Since when did height have to do with growing up?

~~~~~~~~~~~~~~~~~~~

You know you are short when...

The first thing a stranger, you were just introduced to says, "How tall are you?"

What? Do you want my weight and social security number too?

~~~~~~~~~~~~~~~~~~~~~~~~

You know you are short when...

A short person is slightly taller than you and they say, "I feel so tall."

Go figure. I'm glad I can make you feel better about yourself.

~~~~~~~~~~~~~~~~~~~

You know you are short when...

Kids in 5th grade purposely stand next to you sizing you up to see if they are just as tall.

Yes, I stopped growing in 5th grade.

~~~~~~~~~~~~~~~~~~~~~

There are famous people who are short, like Dolly Parton, 5',
Danny DeVito, 5', Michael J. Fox, 5'4", Norene 4'8", Mickey
Rooney 5'3", Zacchaeus was a wee little man, climbed up in a
Sycamore tree to get a good view.

~~~~~~~~~~~~~~~~~~~~

You know you are short when...

You take your kids to the doctor and he says, "Well, they are kind of in the low height range."

Well, hello!

~~~~~~~~~~~~~~~~~~~

You know you are short when...

Your boss's boss pats you on the head.

Should I pant now or later? Bark, bark.

~~~~~~~~~~~~~~~~~~~

You know you are short when...

Someone shouts out, "Oh, my god you're short!"

How observant; thanks for stating the obvious.

~~~~~~~~~~~~~~~~~~

You know you are short when...

You're at work and the supplies you need are too high.

That's where salad serving spoons and forks come in quite handy.

~~~~~~~~~~~~~~~~~~~

You know you are short when...

The copier/fax/scanner machine is as tall as you are.

At least the control panel is just below eye level.

~~~~~~~~~~~~~~~~~~~~~

You know you are short when...

You're over 62, and the doctor's measurement says you shrunk a ½".

Ok, so I don't put that on my driver's license, so what?

~~~~~~~~~~~~~~~~~~~~~~

You know you are short when...

You are 30+, still look young, wearing pony tails, and a door-to-door solicitor asks you if your mother is home. You say, "No."

Ha, well, I didn't lie.

~~~~~~~~~~~~~~~~~~~~~~

You know you are short when...

Someone gawks in unbelief that your kids are taller than you.

Surprise, surprise, surprise!

~~~~~~~~~~~~~~~~~~~~

"We short people have a great perspective on life; we are always looking up.

God makes everything grow to perfection but some things don't take as long."

~~~~~~~~~~~~~~~~~~~

You know you are short when...

People try to bend over or kneel to be your height to take a picture together.

Stand up. You, be you, and I'll be me.

~~~~~~~~~~~~~~~~~~~~

You know you are short when...

Someone bends down to talk to you.

Would you be more comfortable if we both sit in chairs?

~~~~~~~~~~~~~~~~~~~

You know you are short when...

"Friends" nickname you Hobbit.

Do my feet look tough and hairy?

~~~~~~~~~~~~~~~~~~~~

You know you are short when...

Someone talks to you in a baby voice.

Hello, I'm short, not stupid.

~~~~~~~~~~~~~~~~~~~~~~

You know you are short when...

Someone calls you munchkin.

You know you're not in Kansas.

~~~~~~~~~~~~~~~~~~~

You know you are short when...

You're at a party and the person you're talking to suddenly starts up a conversation above your head, with someone standing behind you.

Are we playing monkey in the middle?

~~~~~~~~~~~~~~~~~~~~

"Judge me by my size do you?" Yoda

~~~~~~~~~~~~~~~~~~~~~

You know you are short when...

You're at a grocery store and can't reach the item you want on the top shelf. You ask for help from another nearby customer. All of sudden they straighten out and are a little taller than before.

Thank you. I'm glad you are tall and helpful.

~~~~~~~~~~~~~~~~~~~~

You know you are short when...

Your grandson is nine years old and only has an inch and a half to go before he passes you up.

That's okay, I'm still the grandma.

~~~~~~~~~~~~~~~~~~~~~

You know you are short when...

You get up to address an audience and break the ice by saying; "I'm 4'9" for those who wanted to know and were afraid to ask."

Now they can focus on the topic and not my height.

~~~~~~~~~~~~~~~~~~~~~

You know you are short when...

Someone bumps into you and says, "Oh, I didn't see you down there."

Hello, I'm short, not invisible.

~~~~~~~~~~~~~~~~~~~

You know you are short when...

Someone your age puts their elbow on your shoulder to lean on you.

Excuse me! Do I look like a leaning post?

~~~~~~~~~~~~~~~~~~~~

You know you are short when...

After someone's short comments, she says, "Oh, it looks like you're a little sensitive about your height."

No, it looks like you are a little insensitive about my height.

~~~~~~~~~~~~~~~~~~~

You know you are short when...

You graduate from university with a Master's degree and you are between two very tall people. One of them tries to avoid you. You ask if she is uncomfortable by your height. She says, "yes."

You assure her it's okay. You let her know she can be comfortable because you are.

~~~~~~~~~~~~~~~~~~~

You know you are short when...

You are at a sit-down dinner and the MC introduces you. You stand up next to your chair, and he says, "No really, stand up," and he laughs.

"There's your sign".

~~~~~~~~~~~~~~~~~~~~~~

You know you are short when...

A 250 pound, 6' 2," big, teen guy walks on his knees following you around the grocery store, calling out "mommy, mommy."

It was funny, but who looked like the weird one?

~~~~~~~~~~~~~~~~~~~~

You know you are short when...

Someone says, "For someone so little/short, you really get around and do a lot.

Didn't know there was a height criterion for
doing things for people and community.

~~~~~~~~~~~~~~~~~~~

You know you are short when...

People are sitting down in an auditorium and you want to get up and go to the restroom, most of the time people don't notice you too much.

Because you are almost as tall as they are sitting down.

~~~~~~~~~~~~~~~~~~~

You know you are short when...

You have to use a garden tool to get the laundry out of the washing machine.

Hey, whatever works!

~~~~~~~~~~~~~~~~~~~~

You know you are short when...

The office has gag gifts, and gives you a bicycle flag rod to attach to your body, so they can see your flag coming around the corner.

Ha, ha, Hmmmm, it just might work.

~~~~~~~~~~~~~~~~~~~~

You know you are short when...

You sit behind someone while at your kids/grandkids ballet performance and you cannot see because the person in front of you is sitting taller than you can stand.

You feel like a windshield wiper moving your head
from one side to the other trying to see.

~~~~~~~~~~~~~~~~~~~~~

You know you are short when...

Someone says you are proof that good things come in small packages.

That's the nicest thing someone has ever said to me about my height.

~~~~~~~~~~~~~~~~~~~~

You know you are short when...

A four year old sitting in a cart says, "Why are you so little?"

That's the way God made me.

~~~~~~~~~~~~~~~~~~~

You turn things upside down, as if the potter were thought to be like the clay! Shall what is formed say to the one who formed it, "You did not make me"? Can the pot say to the potter "You know nothing"? Isaiah 29:16 (NIV)

~~~~~~~~~~~~~~~~~~

Yet you, LORD, are our Father.

We are the clay, you are the potter;

we are all the work of your hand. Isaiah 64:8 (NIV)

~~~~~~~~~~~~~~~~~~~~

You know you are short when...

A waitress, at a semi-expensive restaurant, who isn't your waitress, tilts her head, puts her hand on your shoulder, and looks you in the face and says, "You are soooo cute. Your feet dangle and don't even reach the floor."

Thank you for noticing.

~~~~~~~~~~~~~~~~~~~~

You know you are short when...

The counter at the bank is up to your eyes.

Hello, is anybody there?

~~~~~~~~~~~~~~~~~~~~~

You know you are short when...

You go to Disney World with your 6'5" son-in-law, and his stride is three to your one.

Hey, can you give me a piggy back ride?

~~~~~~~~~~~~~~~~~~~~~~

You know you are short when...

Even if the seatbelt is adjusted lower, it still attacks your jugular.

If the airbag don't get ya, the seat belt will.

~~~~~~~~~~~~~~~~~~~~~

You know you are short when...

Clothes (even petite) drag.

That's what tailors are for; ok, just cut off
five inches and we'll be all set.

~~~~~~~~~~~~~~~~~~~

"I'm not short. I'm just unusually not tall."

Short or tall, we all need to beware of our words to others. When people talk to me in a changed voice, it reminds me of when someone speaks louder to someone who cannot speak English well, to try to make them understand. They aren't deaf; they don't know the language.

What is your first reaction when people surprise you with a "short" comment? I have to really think about it when it happens to me. Was I angry, because they made a "short" comment or was it because they insulted my intelligence and character? They don't know me. Why should it matter? I rarely have a comeback when someone makes a short comment, because it always takes me by surprise that someone doesn't see me the way I see me. Do I have to have a comeback?

Live your life. Achieve your goals. Love yourself and others. Many things in life can be changed like weight, looks, character, but generally, you cannot change your height. Being short is who we are. It's up to you and me to make a difference in our own lives and those around us, even the world.

"Even the smallest person can change the course of the future."

J.R.R Tolkien

Printed in the United States
By Bookmasters